AS/A-Level Physical Education

Anatomy & Exercise Physiology

Philip Allan Updates, an imprint of Hodder Education, an Hachette UK company, Market Place, Deddington, Oxfordshire OX15 0SE

Orders

Bookpoint Ltd, 130 Milton Park, Abingdon, Oxfordshire OX14 4SB
tel: 01235 827720   fax: 01235 400454   e-mail: uk.orders@bookpoint.co.uk

Lines are open 9.00 a.m.–5.00 p.m., Monday to Saturday, with a 24-hour message answering service. You can also order through our website: www.philipallan.co.uk

© Philip Allan Updates 2010
ISBN 978-1-4441-1540-6

Impression number   5   4   3   2   1
Year   2014   2013   2012   2011   2010

Printed in Spain

Hachette UK's policy is to use papers that are natural, renewable and recyclable products and made from wood grown in sustainable forests. The logging and manufacturing processes are expected to conform to the environmental regulations of the country of origin.

P01748

Anatomy

Skeleton I

Q1 The skeleton comprises how many bones?

Q2 What are the three main tissues that make up the skeleton?

Q3 Classify the following bones: scapula; femur; vertebra; tarsal.

Q4 Which of the following is not a function of the skeleton: movement; blood production; warmth; protection; support?

ANSWERS

A1 206

A2 Bone; cartilage; ligaments

A3 Flat; long; irregular; short

A4 Warmth

***examiner's* note** A long-term programme of training can strengthen skeletal tissues. In particular, bone density can increase as well as the articular cartilage thickening, which helps prevent wear and tear of the bones. For this reason, physical exercise can be of benefit to women: it helps prevent osteoporosis, a disease associated with brittle bones.

Skeleton II

Q1 Name the five sections of the vertebral column.

Q2 How many pairs of ribs make up the ribcage?

Q3 Which of the following is not part of the axial skeleton: skull; pelvis; spine; ribcage?

Q4 Name the top two bones of the vertebral column. What type of joint exists here?

ANSWERS

A1 Cervical; thoracic; lumbar; sacral; coccygeal

A2 12

A3 The pelvis. This forms part of the appendicular skeleton.

A4 Axis and atlas; pivot joint

examiner's note The size of each vertebral body increases from the cervical vertebrae to the lumbar vertebrae. In this way, the weight of the body can be supported. Most movement of the spine occurs in the cervical and lumbar regions. Note that the vertebral column is s-shaped; this enables it to act as a spring, absorbing shock during running or jumping.

Joint I

Q1 Which structures of the body are responsible for stabilising joints?

Q2 A cartilaginous joint is a type of synovial joint. True or false?

Q3 Give two examples of a hinge joint.

Q4 What movement patterns can be performed at a ball-and-socket joint?

ANSWERS

a place in the body where two
or more bones meet

A1 Ligaments. These are fibrous tissues that join two bones
together

A2 False. A cartilaginous joint allows little movement, while a
synovial joint is freely movable

A3 Any two from: knee; elbow; ankle

A4 Flexion; extension; abduction; adduction; circumduction;
rotation (horizontal abduction, horizontal adduction)

***examiner's* note** Not all joints allow movement. However, for your
examination, you need to focus on those that do, i.e. synovial joints.

(3) ANSWERS

Joint II

Q1 Which bones articulate at the shoulder joint?

Q2 Where in the body might you find a cartilaginous joint?

Q3 What movements can be performed at the radio-ulnar joint?

Q4 What are menisci?

ANSWERS

a place in the body where two or more bones meet

A1 Humerus, scapula (clavicle)

A2 In the lumbar region of the vertebral column

A3 Rotation, pronation, supination

A4 Discs of cartilage found in synovial joints such as the knee which improve the 'fit' between articulating bones and give added protection by preventing wear and tear

***examiner's* note** Synovial joints are classified according to the range and type of movement they allow. You must be able to relate the type of synovial joint to its structure. For example, hinge joints only allow movement in one plane because the intricate network of ligaments crossing the joint restricts movement.

 ANSWERS

Synovial joint

Q1 What name is given to the smooth layer of tissue that covers the ends of the bones at joints?

Q2 What feature of a synovial joint reduces friction between the articulating surfaces of bones and nourishes the articular cartilage?

Q3 What type of synovial joint is the radio-ulnar joint?

Q4 Name two ligaments of the knee joint.

ANSWERS

> a meeting of two or more bones
> where movement is permitted (also
> known as a freely movable joint)

A1 Articular or hyaline cartilage

A2 Synovial fluid

A3 Pivot. This enables pronation and supination of the forearm

A4 Any two from: lateral (collateral); medial (collateral); anterior cruciate; posterior cruciate

***examiner's* note** Extra protection is provided to some synovial joints by discs of cartilage known as menisci, sacs of synovial fluid known as bursae and pads of fat. The knee joint, for example, possesses all three of these protective features because it undergoes tremendous stress during physical activity. The menisci and pads of fat help in shock absorption, while the bursae prevent wear of structures such as ligaments and tendons as they glide past each other.

 ANSWERS

Movement pattern I

Q1 What terms describe movement of a body part (a) towards the midline of the body and (b) away from the midline of the body?

Q2 What action takes place at the knee joint when kicking a football?

Q3 What movement is a combination of flexion, extension, abduction and adduction?

Q4 What is the movement of the trunk that takes place when leaning sideways?

ANSWERS

A1 (a) Adduction
(b) Abduction

A2 Extension

A3 Circumduction; true circumduction, however, can only take place at the ball-and-socket joints of the shoulder and hip

A4 Lateral flexion

***examiner's* note** Movement patterns always come in pairs, since if we can move a body part one way, we must be able to return it to the starting position. Examples include: flexion/extension; abduction/adduction; pronation/supination; dorsiflexion/plantar flexion; lateral rotation/medial rotation; inversion/eversion; elevation/depression.

 ANSWERS

Movement pattern II

Q1 What movement involves the palm of the hand facing upwards?

Q2 What movement takes place at the radio-ulnar joint when performing top spin in tennis?

Q3 Pronation and supination are forms of rotation that occur at the radio-ulnar joint. At what other synovial joints can rotation occur?

Q4 Stand upright. Move your arm up in front of you until it gets to shoulder height. What joint action has taken place? From here, move your arm out sideways. What has now occurred?

ANSWERS

A1 Supination

A2 Pronation

A3 Shoulder, hip and spine

A4 Flexion of the shoulder; horizontal abduction/extension

***examiner's* note** When analysing movement, it is important to identify the starting point and finishing point of the movement. For example, when describing a kicking action at the knee we might say that the action has gone 'from flexion towards extension'. In the 'kick' phase in breaststroke, the femur at the hip moves from an adducted position to an abducted position, returning to an adducted position during recovery.

Movement pattern III

Q1 What action takes place at the ankle during the take-off phase of a high jump?

Q2 Turning of the sole of the foot laterally outwards is known as e................

Q3 What movement pattern does the shoulder undergo when bowling in cricket?

Q4 What joint actions occur at the hip, knee and ankle when driving from the blocks in a sprint start?

ANSWERS

A1 Plantar flexion

A2 Eversion

A3 Circumduction

A4 Hip: extension; knee: extension; ankle: plantarflexion

***examiner's* note** Circumduction is defined as a combination of flexion, extension, abduction and adduction. We might therefore expect that circumduction can occur at the wrist and ankle joints. True circumduction, however, can only occur at the ball-and-socket joints of the shoulder and hip. This is because of the unique structure of ball-and-socket joints, where the rounded head of a bone fits into a cup-shaped cavity, allowing movement in all directions. Ball-and-socket joints also have fewer ligaments, which further increases the movement possible at this type of joint.

 ANSWERS

Muscle function I

Q1 Which muscle group is responsible for exteneee when kicking a football?

Q2 Which muscle is responsible for extension auring a set shot in basketball?

Q3 The a............... d............... is responsible for flexiodder.

Q4 Which muscles cause plantar flexion of the ing the take-off phase in long jump?

ps (rectus femoris and vasti muscles)

rachii

deltoid

emius and soleus

ote Muscles that cause flexion are sometimes called flexors.
use extension are sometimes referred to as extensors. The
ample, causes hip flexion and is known as a hip flexor, while the
s causes extension of the hip and is therefore known as a hip

ERS

Muscle function II

Q1 Which muscle is responsible for extension at the hip when driving out of the blocks in a sprint start?

Q2 In preparation for a block in volleyball, the ankle goes through dorsiflexion. Which muscle is responsible for this?

Q3 Which muscle causes flexion of the hip when performing a pike jump in trampolining?

Q4 The e............... s............... muscles cause extension of the back, e.g. when breathing during the butterfly stroke in swimming.

ANSWERS ▶▶

A1 Gluteus maximus

A2 Tibialis anterior

A3 Iliopsoas

A4 Erector spinae

***examiner's* note** Muscles that cause adduction are called adductors. Muscles that cause abduction are referred to as abductors. For example, the adductor magnus, brevis and longus cause adduction of the hip. The gluteus medius and minimus cause abduction of the hip and are therefore known as abductors.

Origin and insertion

Q1 Give the origin and insertion for the biceps brachii muscle.

Q2 Muscles cannot pull, they can only push. True or false?

Q3 Give the two origins of the deltoid muscle.

Q4 The insertions of the gastrocnemius and soleus are on the same bone. Which bone?

ANSWERS

the ends of a muscle, attached to a
fixed, stable bone (origin) and to a bone
that the muscle moves (insertion)

A1 Scapula; radius

A2 False. Muscles can only pull — they cannot push

A3 Clavicle; scapula

A4 Calcaneus

***examiner's* note** As a rule of thumb, the origin of a muscle is the nearest
flat bone; the insertion is on the bone that the muscle puts into action. For
example, the origin of the rectus femoris (of the quadriceps group) is on the
pelvis (the nearest flat bone), while the insertion is on the tibia (the bone that
it puts into action).

 **ANSWERS**

Antagonistic muscle action

Q1 The muscle that is directly responsible for the movement at a joint is known as the agonist or p............... m................

Q2 During flexion at the elbow, the .... is the agonist while the .... is the antagonist.

Q3 The muscle that stabilises the origin while the agonist contracts is known as a synergist. True or false?

Q4 Name the fixator in the case of flexion at the elbow.

ANSWERS ⟩⟩

the action of muscles working in opposing groups, enabling coordinated movements to take place

A1 Prime mover

A2 Biceps brachii; triceps brachii

A3 False. It is known as a fixator. A synergist is a muscle that prevents any undesired movement

A4 Trapezius

***examiner's* note** Don't forget that the roles of the muscles change. In the above example of elbow flexion, the biceps brachii is the agonist while the triceps brachii is the antagonist. These roles are reversed during elbow extension: the triceps brachii becomes the agonist and the biceps brachii becomes the antagonist. However, since these muscles act over the same joints, the synergist muscle will remain the same.

Muscle contraction

Q1 Identify the type of muscle contraction that takes place in the quadriceps group on landing from a jump shot.

Q2 During the action of throwing a javelin, what type of muscle contraction takes place in the triceps brachii?

Q3 .... contraction can only occur using specialised machinery which keeps the speed of contraction constant.

Q4 During which part of the shot-put action will the muscles of the throwing arm be undergoing isometric contraction?

ANSWERS

A1 Eccentric (isotonic)

A2 Concentric (isotonic)

A3 Isokinetic

A4 When travelling across the circle

examiner's note To determine the type of muscle contraction taking place, you must first establish whether the muscle is shortening (concentric), lengthening (eccentric) or remaining the same length (isometric). During the biceps curl action, you can see the biceps get shorter and fatter during the upward phase. This is concentric contraction. When the bar is lowered under control, the biceps lengthens, undergoing eccentric contraction. When the bar is held steady, with the elbow flexed, for a short period of time, the biceps performs an isometric contraction — it is neither shortening nor lengthening.

Fast-twitch muscle fibre

Q1 Which of the following is not a characteristic of fast-twitch muscle fibre: easily exhausted; doesn't use oxygen; endurance-based; contracts rapidly?

Q2 The type of muscle fibre that is most associated with a shot-putter is fast-twitch g................

Q3 Is capillary density greater on type 2a or type 2b fibres?

Q4 It is possible to convert slow-twitch (type 1) fibres to fast-twitch (type 2) fibres. True or false?

ANSWERS

A1 Endurance-based

A2 Glycolytic

A3 Type 2a fibres, since these pick up certain oxidative (aerobic)
    qualities

A4 False. However, it is possible for fast-twitch (type 2) fibres
    to pick up some characteristics of slow-twitch fibres through
    endurance training. These are known as fast-oxidative, glycolytic
    fibres

examiner's note The relative percentages of fibre types may help in
predicting the physiological potential of an athlete. However, it is only through
hard training that this potential may actually be met.

Slow-twitch muscle fibre

Q1 Slow-twitch motor units have more fibres per motor neurone than fast-twitch fibres. True or false?

Q2 Is the sarcoplasmic reticulum more or less well developed in slow-twitch muscle fibres?

Q3 A slow-twitch fibre has the highest oxidative capacity. True or false?

Q4 The amount of glycogen stored is greatest in fast-twitch muscle fibres. True or false?

ANSWERS

fibre designed for aerobic work, producing low levels of force for long periods of time

A1 False. Slow-twitch motor units have 10–180 fibres per unit whereas fast-twitch motor units have 300–800 fibres per unit

A2 It is less well developed and so releases calcium (which is essential for muscle contraction) more slowly

A3 True. Slow-twitch fibres possess large numbers of mitochondria, which are where aerobic respiration takes place

A4 True. Slow-twitch fibres provide energy by metabolising both fat and glycogen. Fast-twitch fibres only use glycogen and can therefore store more

***examiner's* note** Fast-twitch fibres contract more quickly than slow-twitch fibres largely due to the enzyme ATPase acting more quickly in the former.

 **(15) ANSWERS**

Strengthening exercise 1

Q1 A long-jumper requires strong calf muscles to ensure a powerful drive upwards at take off. What activity could you perform to help strengthen these muscles?

Q2 A bench press is most likely to be used to develop which muscle group?

Q3 Plyometrics is mainly used to develop which muscles?

Q4 A press-up will help strengthen which of the muscles acting over the elbow joints?

ANSWERS

an activity used to improve the strength of muscles or muscle groups

A1 Calf raises

A2 Pectorals (pectoralis major, pectoralis minor)

A3 Quadriceps group, hamstrings group and calf muscles; but some exercises can be used to develop muscles of the upper body

A4 Triceps brachii

***examiner's* note** There are three types of strength: maximum strength, elastic strength and strength endurance. When developing a strength training programme, you must first decide which type of strength you are trying to improve. For the development of maximum strength, you would use a high load with few repetitions. The development of strength endurance involves sessions of low resistance, with many repetitions required.

Strengthening exercise II

Q1 In order to strengthen the latissimus dorsi muscle you might perform c............-u............

Q2 Which muscles are strengthened using a hip abductor machine?

Q3 When performing the shot-put, a sharp snap of the wrist is needed upon release of the shot. What exercise could you perform to strengthen the muscles of the forearm?

Q4 A 'Swiss ball' is designed to strengthen and improve the 'core stability' of which group of muscles?

ANSWERS

an activity used to improve the strength
of muscles or muscle groups

A1 Chin-ups

A2 Gluteus medius and gluteus minimus

A3 Wrist curls

A4 Abdominals, transverse abdominis, erector spinae and multifidus

examiner's **note** Following strength training, muscle fibres adapt by
increasing in size. This is known as muscle fibre hypertrophy. Strength gains will
also result from the recruitment of more motor units.

Core stability

Q1 Name the deep muscle of the core that helps to stabilise the cartilaginous joints of the spine.

Q2 Give two methods of improving core stability.

Q3 Name the muscle of the core that helps to stabilise the lower spine and pelvis during physical activity.

Q4 The rectus abdominus muscle is a key muscle of core stability. True or false?

ANSWERS

the combined strength of all the muscles of the trunk

A1 The multifidus

A2 Any two from: the plank; exercises using a 'Swiss ball'; crunches; reverse sit-ups

A3 Transverse abdominis

A4 False. Although the rectus abdominus may contribute to core stability, its primary function is to enable flexion of the trunk

***examiner's* note** The benefits of improving core stability are numerous for sports performers. It can enable the working muscles to generate more forces as they have a firm base against which to pull, it can improve posture and technique and it reduces the risk of injury.

Anatomy of the heart

Q1 Name the structure of the heart that divides it into right and left sides.

Q2 The a................ valves separate the upper and lower chambers of the heart.

Q3 The blood from the left ventricle leaves the heart via this major artery.

Q4 Give two functions of the valves of the heart.

ANSWERS

the complex structure enabling the
heart to fulfil its dual role of oxygen
delivery and removal of waste

A1 Septum

A2 Atrioventricular

A3 Aorta

A4 To ensure that blood flows through the heart in one direction;
to prevent backflow of blood within the heart

***examiner's* note** Make sure that you can trace the path of blood through
the heart and that you are able to name the structures of the heart that the
blood goes through on its journey. It is a good idea to link this to the cardiac
cycle.

Blood vessels of the heart

Q1 Which blood vessels carry oxygenated blood from the lungs to the heart?

Q2 The main veins of the body that return oxygen-poor blood to the heart are the v............... c...............

Q3 The blood vessels that supply the heart muscle itself (myocardium) with blood are known as what?

Q4 Does the pulmonary artery carry oxygen-rich or oxygen-poor blood?

ANSWERS

a system of channels enabling blood to flow to, from and through the heart

A1 Pulmonary veins

A2 Venae cavae

A3 Coronary arteries

A4 Oxygen-poor blood. The pulmonary artery takes deoxygenated blood from the right ventricle to the lungs

examiner's **note** The heart is a muscle itself and therefore requires its own supply of blood, which provides oxygen and other necessary nutrients. This is known as coronary circulation and is carried out by the coronary arteries. Sometimes the coronary arteries become blocked, starving part of the heart of oxygen and leading to a heart attack. Regular aerobic exercise can prevent this from happening.

Conduction system of the heart

Q1 What term is used to describe the ability of the heart to generate its own impulses? The heart is m................ .

Q2 The pacemaker of the heart is known as the AV node. True or false?

Q3 What is the function of the Purkinje fibres during a heartbeat?

Q4 The nerves within the septum of the heart are known as the Bundle of Hers. True or false?

ANSWERS

A1 Myogenic

A2 False. The pacemaker of the heart is the SA node. The AV node spreads the impulse throughout the ventricles, enabling them to contract

A3 They help spread the impulse rapidly to all areas of the ventricles so that they contract more or less at the same time

A4 False. These nerves are known as the Bundle of His

***examiner's* note** In the examination, try to link the conduction system of the heart with the cardiac cycle. The two are inextricably linked. This will also help you to explain and trace the path of blood through the heart, which is essential knowledge for your examination.

Cardiac cycle

Q1 What stage of the cardiac cycle takes place when the atria fill with blood?

Q2 Place the following in the correct sequential order: atrial systole; ventricular diastole; ventricular systole; atrial diastole.

Q3 The term 'systole' refers to periods of contraction of the heart. True or false?

Q4 The e_____ f_____ is the percentage of blood pumped out of the heart with each beat.

ANSWERS

A1 Atrial diastole

A2 Atrial diastole; ventricular diastole; atrial systole; ventricular
systole

A3 True

A4 Ejection fraction

***examiner's* note** For maximum marks in your exam, you must link the
events of the cardiac cycle to the conduction system of the heart. The ejection
fraction is the proportion of the blood in the left ventricle that is actually
pumped out. It can be calculated by dividing the stroke volume by the end
diastolic volume and multiplying it by 100.

Autonomic nervous system

Q1 Name the two divisions of the autonomic nervous system.

Q2 The parasympathetic system controls bodily functions during normal resting conditions. True or false?

Q3 The sympathetic nervous system causes an increase in heart rate during exercise. It does this by releasing a................

Q4 To help return the heart rate to resting levels following exercise, the parasympathetic system responds to information from b................

ANSWERS

a subdivision of the nervous system
controlling aspects of body functioning
not under conscious control

A1 The sympathetic and the parasympathetic systems

A2 True. The sympathetic system tends to operate during exercise and situations of stress

A3 Adrenaline (and noradrenaline)

A4 Baroreceptors

***examiner's* note** The sympathetic and parasympathetic nervous systems act upon the cardiac control centre, which is located in the medulla oblongata of the brain. The cardiac control centre then relays information to the sino-atrial node, which is situated in the heart, instructing it to speed up or slow down the rate at which the heart beats.

Neural control of the heart

Q1 Name two types of receptor that stimulate the cardiac control centre.

Q2 In order to speed up heart rate, the sympathetic nerve stimulates the s............-a............ node.

Q3 Name the main parasympathetic nerve.

Q4 Prior to exercise, there is a slight elevation in heart rate called the anticipatory rise. Why does this happen?

ANSWERS

A1 Any two from: proprioceptors; mechanoreceptors; chemoreceptors; baroreceptors; thermoreceptors

A2 Sino-atrial

A3 Vagus nerve

A4 To prepare the body for the imminent exercise, the sympathetic nervous system releases adrenaline and noradrenaline. These increase the heart rate even though exercise has yet to start

examiner's note The sympathetic and parasympathetic nervous systems interact to speed up the heart rate prior to and during exercise and return the heart rate to resting levels following exercise.

Stroke volume

Q1 What is the average stroke volume for a male at rest?

Q2 H............. is the term used to describe an enlarged heart following training.

Q3 Does stroke volume increase or decrease during exercise? Explain your answer.

Q4 What term is used to describe the proportion of blood pumped out of the left ventricle after each contraction?

ANSWERS

the volume of blood pumped out of the heart (left ventricle) per beat

A1 Between 70 ml and 80 ml, although some endurance athletes may have a resting value of around 100 ml

A2 Hypertrophy

A3 It increases due to the stretching of the cardiac fibres of the heart (Starling's law)

A4 Ejection fraction

***examiner's* note** Following training, the stroke volume of a strength athlete increases as a result of a thicker heart muscle (myocardium); that of an endurance athlete increases due to a greater ventricular volume. Ejection fraction is determined by dividing the stroke volume by the end diastolic volume, expressed as a percentage.

Heart rate

Q1 What term is used to describe a resting heart rate of below 60 bpm?

Q2 What is the average resting heart rate of an adult?

Q3 For what would you use the calculation '220 minus age'?

Q4 Some elite endurance athletes have recorded resting heart rates of below 30 bpm. This is because their hearts enlarge as a result of all the training they undertake. This is known as c............ h.................

ANSWERS

the number of times the ventricles of the heart contract in 1 minute

A1 Bradycardia

A2 72 bpm (although anywhere between 70 bpm and 80 bpm is acceptable)

A3 To calculate the maximum heart rate (HR_{max}) of an individual

A4 Cardiac hypertrophy

***examiner's* note** The relationship between heart rate, stroke volume and cardiac output is an important one to remember:

cardiac output (Q) = stroke volume (SV) × heart rate (HR)

During exercise, cardiac output can rise dramatically due to increases in both stroke volume and heart rate. This ensures that there is a plentiful supply of blood transporting oxygen and glucose to the working muscles.

Cardiac output

Q1 Cardiac output is dependent upon two variables. What are they and what is their relationship?

Q2 The resting cardiac output of an athlete is greater than that of a non-athlete. True or false?

Q3 (a) Give the typical cardiac output for a male at rest.
(b) By how much might this be increased during exercise?

Q4 Cardiac output increases in direct proportion to exercise intensity. True or false?

ANSWERS

the volume of blood pumped out of the heart per minute

A1 Stroke volume and heart rate
cardiac output (Q) = stroke volume (SV) × heart rate (HR)

A2 False. Resting cardiac output will be the same. Only while exercising will the cardiac output of an athlete be greater than that of a non-athlete

A3 (a) Approximately 5 litres/min; (b) between 20 and 40 litres/min, depending on the endurance capacity of the individual

A4 True. It increases linearly with exercise intensity until it reaches the point of maximal cardiac output (Q_{max}); it then plateaus

***examiner's* note** During exercise, the cardiac output rises to increase the speed at which carbon dioxide and other metabolites are removed from the body, as well as to supply the working muscles with greater amounts of oxygen.

Venous return

Q1 The relationship between cardiac output and venous return is known as S............ l............

Q2 When we exercise, muscles help squeeze blood back towards the heart. What is this mechanism known as?

Q3 What structures prevent backflow of blood within the veins?

Q4 Venous return during exercise is aided by pressure changes in the thoracic cavity resulting from an increase in the rate and depth of breathing. This is known as the r............ p............

ANSWERS

the process by which the blood returns to the right side of the heart via the veins

A1 Starling's law

A2 Muscle pump

A3 Pocket valves

A4 Respiratory pump

examiner's note Performing a cool-down following training helps to maintain the venous return mechanism. This helps to prevent the dizziness associated with stopping exercise abruptly and to disperse lactic acid. The lactic acid is broken down into water and carbon dioxide, which can then be removed from the body through expiration (i.e. breathed out).

Blood

Q1 Give two functions of the blood that are of primary importance during exercise.

Q2 The relative thickness of the blood and its resistance to flow is known as its v................

Q3 Name two constituents of the blood.

Q4 The regulation of pH (acidity) by the blood is known as b................

ANSWERS

A1 Any two from: transportation of nutrients; temperature
regulation; pH regulation

A2 Viscosity

A3 Any two from: plasma; red blood cells (erythrocytes); white
blood cells (leucocytes); platelets (thrombocytes)

A4 Buffering

***examiner's* note** The average male has a total blood volume of 5–6 litres;
the average female blood volume is approximately 4–5 litres. Aerobic training
can increase these blood volumes by up to 30%.

(29) ANSWERS

Double circulatory system

Q1 The right side of the heart deals with oxygenated blood. True or false?

Q2 The term 's_____' refers to blood that is pumped from the left ventricle to all of the body's tissues.

Q3 What does the term 'pulmonary' usually refer to?

Q4 The pulmonary vein carries oxygenated blood. True or false?

ANSWERS ▶▶

the transport of blood (a) between
heart and lungs and (b) between
heart and other body tissues

A1 False. The right side of the heart pumps blood low in oxygen to the lungs to be reoxygenated

A2 Systemic

A3 The lungs; e.g. the pulmonary blood vessels connect the heart with the lungs

A4 True. The pulmonary vein transports oxygenated blood from the lungs back to the heart

examiner's note The unique structure of the heart enables it to function as a dual-action pump. The septum divides the heart into right and left sides, which means that the right side can pump deoxygenated blood to the lungs while the left side can circulate oxygenated blood around the rest of the body.

Blood vessels I

Q1 Blood vessels that typically carry oxygenated blood are a............... and a...............

Q2 Capillaries are the sites for gaseous exchange. How does the structure of the capillaries allow this?

Q3 V............... is a reduction in size of the lumen of the arterioles.

Q4 What are the structures found in veins that prevent the backflow of blood?

ANSWERS

A1 Arteries; arterioles

A2 The walls of capillaries are only one cell thick. This allows efficient exchange of oxygen and carbon dioxide

A3 Vasoconstriction

A4 Pocket valves. These also help in the return of the blood to the heart (the venous return mechanism)

examiner's note The only arteries that carry deoxygenated blood are the pulmonary arteries; these carry deoxygenated blood from the right side of the heart to the lungs, where it can be oxygenated once again. The only veins that carry oxygenated blood are the pulmonary veins; these carry the freshly oxygenated blood from the lungs to the left side of the heart, from where it can be pumped around the entire body.

Blood vessels II

Q1 The total cross-sectional area of the capillaries is greater than that of the aorta. True or false?

Q2 What type of muscle is found in the walls of blood vessels?

Q3 The structures that regulate the flow of blood into capillaries are known as p............... s................

Q4 The process of controlling the diameter of arteries is known as venomotor control. True or false?

ANSWERS ▶▶

A1 True. This accounts for the relatively low blood pressure in the capillaries

A2 Smooth muscle

A3 Pre-capillary sphincters

A4 False. It is vasomotor control. Venomotor control refers to the control of the diameter of veins

***examiner's* note** The blood vessels form a continuous network, which creates a double circuit connecting the heart to the lungs and to all other body tissues. The function of the blood vessels is not only to carry blood around the body, but also to help in the redistribution of blood during exercise. They do this by means of the vascular shunt.

Blood pressure

Q1 State the two variables that determine blood pressure.

Q2 Blood pressure is highest in the capillaries. True or false?

Q3 What instrument is used to measure blood pressure? Give the typical blood pressure for a male at rest.

Q4 Which type of exercise causes the greatest increase in blood pressure: aerobic or anaerobic?

ANSWERS

A1 Cardiac output (blood flow) and resistance to blood flow by the blood vessels

A2 False. Blood pressure is greatest in the aorta and decreases with distance from the heart

A3 Sphygmomanometer (or a digital blood pressure recorder); 120 mmHg/80 mmHg

A4 Anaerobic

***examiner's* note** During aerobic, continuous-type exercise, blood pressure may not rise significantly, but during bouts of high-intensity anaerobic exercise, both systolic and diastolic pressure increase.

Mechanics of breathing I

Q1 Which two muscles are responsible for inspiration at rest?

Q2 When the chest expands during inspiration, does the pressure within the lungs increase or decrease?

Q3 Expiration is a passive process at rest. But which muscles are responsible for expiration during exercise?

Q4 During expiration, the diaphragm contracts downwards and flattens. True or false?

ANSWERS

A1 External intercostal muscles and the diaphragm

A2 It decreases. This creates a pressure differential between the inside and outside the body and causes air to rush into the lungs to equalise the pressures inside and outside the body

A3 Internal intercostal muscles and abdominals (rectus abdominis, transverse abdominis)

A4 False. It relaxes into a dome shape

***examiner's* note** You must be able to state which muscles are responsible for inspiration and expiration. Think opposites: external intercostals are needed for inspiration; internal intercostals are needed for expiration.

Mechanics of breathing II

Q1 Other than the external intercostal muscles and diaphragm, which muscles are recruited during exercise to aid inspiration?

Q2 What happens to the pressure within the lungs during expiration?

Q3 Are the external or internal intercostal muscles recruited for expiration during exercise?

Q4 During expiration the diaphragm is forced upwards into the shape of a dome. True or false?

ANSWERS

A1 Sternocleidomastoid, scaleni, pectoralis minor

A2 It increases to a point where it becomes higher than atmospheric pressure. This causes air to rush out of the lungs until equilibrium is reached

A3 Internal intercostal muscles

A4 True

***examiner's* note** For your examination, it is wise to link the mechanics of breathing to the structures involved in neural control, such as chemoreceptors, proprioceptors, thermoreceptors and baroreceptors.

Control of breathing

Q1 The areas that regulate breathing are collectively called the
r............... c............... c................

Q2 What are the two parts of the respiratory centre?

Q3 The muscles under the control of the inspiratory centre are the
diaphragm and the internal intercostal muscles. True or false?

Q4 Name two types of receptor that act upon the inspiratory
centre.

ANSWERS

A1 Respiratory control centre

A2 The inspiratory and the expiratory centres. These regulate
inspiration and expiration respectively

A3 False. The muscles under the control of the inspiratory centre
are the diaphragm and the external intercostal muscles

A4 Any two from: chemoreceptor; proprioceptor; thermoreceptor

***examiner's* note** Over-inflation of the lungs is prevented by the Hering–
Breuer reflex. This stops the action of the inspiratory centre and stimulates the
expiratory centre to initiate expiration.

Partial pressure

Q1 Gases always move from areas of high pressure to areas of low pressure. True or false?

Q2 Is the partial pressure of oxygen in alveolar air higher or lower than that in the capillaries surrounding the alveoli?

Q3 The term used to describe the movement of a gas across a membrane is known as d................

Q4 Does the oxygen diffusion capacity increase, decrease or remain the same as exercise commences?

ANSWERS

the pressure exerted by an individual gas when it exists within a mixture of gases

A1 True. Gases always move from high to low partial pressure, until equilibrium is reached

A2 Higher. This ensures that oxygen moves from the alveoli into the bloodstream

A3 Diffusion

A4 Increases. This is largely due to an increase in cardiac output and elevated blood pressure

***examiner's* note** Carbon dioxide diffuses more easily than oxygen despite having a smaller pressure gradient, as it is up to 20 times more soluble than oxygen and can therefore move across a membrane more easily.

(37) **ANSWERS**

Effects of altitude

Q1 Does the relative percentage of oxygen in the atmosphere increase, decrease or stay the same with an increase in altitude?

Q2 Does partial pressure of oxygen decrease with altitude?

Q3 Does the pressure gradient between the blood and the tissues decrease with altitude?

Q4 Which is least likely to increase with altitude: respiratory rate, heart rate, VO_2 max or cardiac output?

ANSWERS

the influences on physiology of hypobaric (low atmospheric pressure) environments

A1 It stays the same. The relative percentages of gases do not change. It is the overall pressure of the air and therefore the partial pressures of individual gases that decrease with altitude

A2 Yes

A3 Yes. A reduced pressure gradient means that there is a decreased movement of oxygen from the blood into the tissues

A4 VO_2max — it decreases with altitude

***examiner's* note** Prolonged exposure to altitude can cause some adaptation of the body, typically an improvement in the oxygen-carrying capacity of the blood due to an increase in the volume of the red blood cells.

Haemoglobin

Q1 What is the formula HbO_2 better known as?

Q2 Approximately what percentage of carbon dioxide produced during exercise combines with haemoglobin?

Q3 Approximately how much oxygen is carried by haemoglobin?

Q4 Give two factors that cause the dissociation of oxygen from haemoglobin.

ANSWERS

A1 Oxyhaemoglobin

A2 20%

A3 97%

A4 Any two from: increased carbon dioxide production; increased body temperature; decreased muscle pH

***examiner's* note** Blood is the main means of transport in the body — as well as being the main conduit for nutrients and hormones, it is responsible for the delivery of oxygen to working muscles and the removal of carbon dioxide from muscles. Each molecule of haemoglobin can combine with four molecules of oxygen, thus making the transport of oxygen very efficient.

Oxyhaemoglobin dissociation curve

Q1 At the lungs, approximately how much of the haemoglobin is saturated with oxygen?

Q2 What factors cause a reduction in the saturation of haemoglobin with oxygen during exercise?

Q3 What happens to the oxyhaemoglobin dissociation curve during exercise?

Q4 What is the effect of the Bohr shift?

ANSWERS

a curve that represents the amount of
haemoglobin saturated with oxygen as
the blood circulates through the body

A1 97%

A2 An increased blood acidity (fall in pH), increased CO_2 content,
increased lactic acid production, increased body/muscle
temperature

A3 It shifts to the right

A4 It frees up more oxygen, which can subsequently be used by the
working muscles

***examiner's* note** During exercise, the shift in the oxyhaemoglobin curve
to the right is due to an increased release of oxygen to the working muscles.
Following exercise however, the increase in blood pH and decrease in pCO_2
and body temperature cause the curve to return to its resting position by
shifting to the left.

 ANSWERS

Lung volumes

Q1 (a) Which two variables are used to calculate minute ventilation?
(b) State the equation that describes their relationship.
(c) What are the typical resting values of these variables?

Q2 Does inspiratory reserve volume increase with exercise?

Q3 What piece of equipment is used to measure lung volumes?

Q4 Tidal volume is the volume of air inspired and expired per breath. True or false?

ANSWERS

A1 (a) Tidal volume; frequency of breathing
    (b) minute ventilation (VE) = tidal volume (TV) × frequency (F)
    (c) TV = 500 ml; F = 15/min (therefore VE = 7.5 litres/min)

A2 No. It decreases to enable tidal volume to increase during exercise

A3 A spirometer

A4 False. Tidal volume is the volume of air inspired *or* expired per breath

***examiner's* note** You must ensure that when asked to state a volume, you give the correct units. Lung volumes are typically measured in litres or dm^3, and sometimes you are required to quantify your answer by stating a time period, such as 'per minute'.

Smoking

Q1 Name the gas contained in cigarette smoke that reduces the availability of oxygen to the tissues.

Q2 Smoking causes the heart rate to increase, even at rest. True or false?

Q3 Smoking can cause a reduction in VO_2max (the maximum volume of oxygen utilised by the muscles) by approximately how much?

Q4 What substance can coat the respiratory structures, hindering gaseous exchange?

ANSWERS

A1 Carbon monoxide

A2 True. The heart must work harder in order to compensate for the reduced transportation of oxygen

A3 10%

A4 Tar

***examiner's* note** Oxygen has a high affinity for haemoglobin. However, carbon monoxide's affinity for haemoglobin is about 250 times greater than that of oxygen and so binds preferentially to it.

Healthy, balanced lifestyle

Q1 Give two health-related consequences of smoking.

Q2 Exercise can improve the functioning of the cardiovascular system. One way is through the enlargement of the heart. This is more correctly known as what?

Q3 The strength of skeletal tissues such as bones improves following an exercise programme. What accounts for this increase in strength?

Q4 One negative impact of stress on the health of an individual is hypertension. Explain what is meant by 'hypertension'.

ANSWERS

A1 Any two from: restricted oxygen transport; narrowing of
respiratory airways; deposition of tar; cardiovascular disease;
coronary heart disease; lung cancer; emphysema

A2 Cardiac hypertrophy

A3 Bone density increases (new bone cells are laid down along the
new lines of stress experienced during exercise)

A4 Hypertension is high blood pressure that is consistently over
160 mmHg/95 mmHg

examiner's note Aerobic exercise can reduce the overall risk of developing
forms of cardiovascular disease by approximately 30%, largely due to the
adaptation of the cardiovascular system. These adaptations include cardiac
hypertrophy, enhanced elasticity of the arteries/arterioles and reduced blood
viscosity.

Response to exercise I

Q1 What happens to the inspiratory reserve volume during exercise? Does it increase, decrease or remain the same?

Q2 At rest, only 20% of the cardiac output is distributed to the working muscles. By how much can this rise during exercise: 55%; 65%; 75%; 85%?

Q3 Blood and muscle pH increases during exercise. True or false?

Q4 During exercise, there is an increase in the $a\text{-}vO_2\,\text{diff}$. What does $a\text{-}vO_2\,\text{diff}$ stand for?

ANSWERS

the immediate response of the body to exercise

A1 It decreases, thus enabling tidal volume to increase

A2 85% (depending upon the intensity of the exercise)

A3 False. Increases in acidity cause the pH of the muscle and blood to decrease

A4 Arterio-venous oxygen difference — it is a measure of oxygen consumption

***examiner's* note** Immediately prior to exercise, a slight increase in the resting heart rate of a performer might be observed. This occurs as a result of an increase in the activity of the sympathetic nervous system, which releases adrenaline to help the body cope when exercise begins, and is known as the anticipatory rise.

Response to exercise II

Q1 The process of blood redistribution that occurs during exercise is known as the v............... s...............

Q2 Which helps speed up blood flow to the working muscles during exercise: vasoconstriction or vasodilation?

Q3 S............ l............ helps to explain the increase in stroke volume that accompanies exercise.

Q4 There is little change in blood pressure during aerobic exercise involving large muscle groups. True or false?

ANSWERS

the immediate response of the body to exercise

A1 Vascular shunt

A2 Vasoconstriction

A3 Starling's law

A4 True, but there are significant increases in blood pressure during very high-intensity exercise or during activities that require isometric muscle contractions

***examiner's* note** At rest, about 70% of the total blood volume is found in the veins. This provides a large reservoir of blood which is returned rapidly to the heart when exercise commences. Since cardiac output is dependent on venous return (Starling's law), this ensures a large cardiac output even at the beginning of exercise.

 **45** ANSWERS

Hormone

Q1 Which hormone accounts for the increased muscle mass in males?

Q2 Give two actions of adrenaline.

Q3 What term is used to describe the slight elevation in heart rate prior to exercise, resulting from the action of adrenaline?

Q4 The hormone responsible for fat deposition and regulation of the menstrual cycle in females is o................

ANSWERS

a chemical substance produced and released in the body, with a particular function and target tissue

A1 Testosterone

A2 Any two from: increases the force of muscular contraction; increases the metabolic rate; increases release of glucose and free fatty acids into the bloodstream; redistributes blood during exercise

A3 Anticipatory rise

A4 Oestrogen. This accounts for the higher body fat composition in females compared with males

***examiner's* note** Release of the adrenal hormones is from the adrenal medullae, which are situated at the top of the kidneys. These are stimulated by sympathetic nerves when exercise commences and can increase heart rate.

Types of motion

Q1 What is general motion?

Q2 What type of force is required to produce angular motion?

Q3 Define the term 'direct force'.

Q4 A swimmer primarily exhibits which type of motion?

ANSWERS ▶▶

A1 A combination of linear and angular motion

A2 An eccentric force

A3 A force that is applied through the centre of mass of a body or object

A4 General motion — the trunk moves linearly because of the angular movements of the arms and legs

***examiner's* note** Most motion in sport is general motion — a combination of linear and angular types. Pure linear motion is rarely seen but examples include waterskiing and tobogganing. Linear motion can also take place along a curved path, as with a projectile in flight — this is known as curvilinear motion.

Newton's laws of motion

Q1 Newton's first law of motion is also known as the law of i.............

Q2 Newton's second law of motion is also known as the law of a.............

Q3 Newton's third law of motion is also known as the law of r.............

Q4 A rugby ball placed on a kicking tee and waiting to be struck relates to which of Newton's laws?

ANSWERS))

A1 Inertia

A2 Acceleration

A3 Reaction

A4 First

***examiner's* note** Newton's laws can be used to explain all movements within sport. For example, a sprinter will experience Newton's first law of motion when in the blocks awaiting the gun. When the gun sounds, the third law of motion will operate: when the sprinter pushes down and backwards onto the starting blocks, the blocks push the athlete forwards and upwards. As the sprinter accelerates out of the blocks, the acceleration is proportional to the force produced by the leg muscles, and takes place in the direction in which the force acts. This is Newton's second law.

Centre of mass

Q1 Is the centre of mass of an athlete in a fixed position?

Q2 Where does the centre of mass lie for a high jumper performing a Fosbury flop?

Q3 When performing a handstand, the gymnast's centre of mass should lie outside her base of support. True or false?

Q4 A high diver performing a front somersault applies a force that passes outside his centre of mass. In doing so, he initiates rotation. This is known as an e............... force.

ANSWERS ▶▶

the point at which the body is balanced in all directions

A1 No. The centre of mass will move depending on the relative position of body parts

A2 Outside the body. Thus it is actually possible for the centre of mass to travel under the bar while the high jumper goes over it!

A3 False. In order to maintain balance, the centre of mass should be over and within the gymnast's base of support

A4 Eccentric

examiner's note For symmetrical (including spherical) objects, the centre of mass can be located at the geometric centre.

Lever system

Q1 Identify the three components of a lever system.

Q2 During the take-off phase of a long jump, which type of lever system is in operation at the ankle?

Q3 What term is used to describe the relative efficiency of a lever system?

Q4 Which lever system is in operation at the elbow during a biceps curl?

ANSWERS

A1 Fulcrum; effort; load (resistance)

A2 A second-class lever system

A3 Mechanical advantage/disadvantage

A4 A third-class lever system

examiner's note To determine the class of lever in operation, you must first decide which component is in the middle. For a first-class lever, this will be the fulcrum; for a second-class lever, it will be the load; for a third-class lever, it will be the effort. Some lever systems are able to overcome a heavy load; others can help impart velocity to an object.

Energy system I

Q1 With which energy system would you associate the electron transport system?

Q2 Which of the following would get energy solely from splitting ATP: 50 m swimmer; 1000 m sprint cyclist; shot-putter?

Q3 When one molecule of glucose is completely downgraded, sufficient energy is released to resynthesise 38 molecules of ATP. True or false?

Q4 Name the predominant food fuels used during a triathlon.

ANSWERS ▶▶

a process of energy production in the body for ATP resynthesis

A1 Aerobic

A2 Shot-putter — there is sufficient ATP in the body for about 3 seconds of maximal exercise; a shot-put lasts for approximately 3 seconds and therefore will not require any phosphocreatine

A3 True. Two via the lactic acid system and 36 via the aerobic system

A4 Fatty acids and glycogen — the longer the duration of the activity, the more we rely on stores of fat as fuel

***examiner's* note** To determine the energy system in operation, you must first consider the intensity and duration of the activity concerned. The higher the intensity, the more we rely on anaerobic systems. Longer-duration activities assume lower intensity and therefore rely on the aerobic energy system.

Energy system II

Q1 A............. g............. is an alternative term for the lactic acid pathway.

Q2 What term is given to the point at which one energy system becomes exhausted and another becomes more dominant?

Q3 Which enzyme is responsible for the breakdown of adenosine triphosphate (ATP)?

Q4 Which of the following will not use the lactic acid system: gymnast doing a floor routine; squash player during a rally; basketball player during a full court press; spin bowler in cricket?

ANSWERS

a process of energy production in the body for ATP resynthesis

A1 Anaerobic glycolysis

A2 Threshold, e.g. the ATP/PC–lactic acid threshold occurs between 8 and 10 seconds

A3 ATPase

A4 Spin bowler — all the other activities are of higher intensity and longer duration

***examiner's* note** Training can improve the relative efficiency of each energy system. However, it is essential that all training is tailor-made to meet the requirements of the activity (specificity). For example, a sprinter will improve the efficiency of the ATP/PC system by performing sprint interval training, while the aerobic system of an endurance athlete will be enhanced through continuous training.

Food fuel

Q1 What are the three main energy-providing nutrients?

Q2 Glycogen depletion is greatest during high-intensity exercise. True or false?

Q3 The process that converts fatty acids into acetyl coA is known as b............... o...............

Q4 The amount of energy gained from 1 g of glycogen and 1 g of fat is the same. True or false?

ANSWERS

respiratory substrate used in the production of energy required to resynthesise ATP

A1 Carbohydrates (glycogen); fats (fatty acids); proteins (amino acids)

A2 True

A3 Beta oxidation

A4 False. 1 g of fat can generate 2.25 times as much energy as a similar amount of glycogen, but it requires substantially more oxygen to release the energy stored within it

***examiner's* note** Duration and intensity of exercise play a significant role in the type of food fuel we use. Fats are the primary fuel source during low-intensity exercise due to the recruitment of slow-twitch muscle fibres, which possess more fat-metabolising enzymes (lipases). However, the complete oxidation of fat is dependent on the breakdown of glycogen — 'fats only burn in the flame of carbohydrate'. Higher-intensity exercise (above 60% of VO_2max) relies more heavily on carbohydrates.

Glycogen

Q1 Approximately how much of the daily caloric intake should be carbohydrate, to ensure normal muscle glycogen levels?

Q2 Slow-twitch fibres (type 1) rely solely on glycogen as an energy source. True or false?

Q3 Where in the body is glycogen stored?

Q4 H............... t............... w............... is attributed to muscle glycogen depletion during endurance events.

ANSWERS

the stored form of carbohydrate that is converted to glucose and broken down to release energy

A1 At least 50%, although endurance athletes may need a higher proportion, perhaps in the region of 55–65% of caloric intake

A2 False. Slow-twitch fibres will also metabolise fatty acids

A3 In the muscles and liver

A4 Hitting the wall

examiner's note The total store of glycogen in the body is about 375 g, of which 250 g are stored as muscle glycogen, 110 g are stored in the liver and 15 g are found in blood plasma as blood glucose. This should fuel exercise at low intensity for approximately 90 minutes.

ATP/PC (alactic) system

Q1 Which enzyme is responsible for the breakdown of phosphocreatine (creatine phosphate)?

Q2 What term describes the process of linked chemical reactions?

Q3 The ATP/PC energy system is used in activities of high intensity and relatively short duration. True or false?

Q4 State the equations that summarise the ATP/PC system (hint: three separate equations are needed).

ANSWERS

A1 Creatine kinase

A2 Coupled reaction

A3 True; this is due to the relative ease with which the energy stored within phosphocreatine can be accessed

A4 ATP → ADP + P$_i$ + energy
PC → P + C + energy
energy + ADP + P$_i$ → ATP

***examiner's* note** Some athletes seek to improve the efficiency of their ATP/PC system through creatine supplementation. The aim of ingesting creatine monohydrate is to boost muscular stores of phosphocreatine and extend the duration of this system, but the jury is still out as to the overall effectiveness of this ergogenic aid.

Lactic acid system

Q1 Name the intermediary substance derived from glycogen in the process of forming pyruvic acid.

Q2 What does PFK stand for?

Q3 There is a net gain of two molecules of ATP in the lactic acid system. True or false?

Q4 The enzyme responsible for converting pyruvic acid into lactic acid is l............ d............

ANSWERS

reactions in cells that release energy
from glycogen in the absence of
oxygen to resynthesise ATP

A1 Glucose-6-phosphate

A2 Phosphofructokinase (an enzyme used to initiate glycolysis in the
lactic acid pathway)

A3 True

A4 Lactate dehydrogenase

***examiner's* note** The lactic acid system actually provides sufficient energy to
resynthesise three molecules of ATP, but the process of glycolysis itself requires
energy (one molecule of ATP) — hence the net gain of two molecules of ATP.

Lactic acid

Q1 What do we call the point at which lactic acid begins to accumulate in the blood?

Q2 Which of these is likely to result in large amounts of lactic acid: a marathon run; 100 m sprint; 200 m swim; gymnastics vault?

Q3 Increases in lactic acid result in increases in muscle pH. True or false?

Q4 One way in which the body deals with lactic acid production is through b................

ANSWERS

a by-product of anaerobic glycolysis
— pyruvic acid is converted into lactic
acid in the absence of oxygen

A1 Onset of blood lactate accumulation (OBLA)

A2 200 m swim, although some lactic acid will be produced in each of the other activities

A3 False. Muscle pH will decrease with increased acidity

A4 Buffering

***examiner's* note** Although the terms 'lactic acid' and 'lactate' are often used interchangeably, they are different compounds. Lactate is a salt of lactic acid, produced when lactic acid releases hydrogen ions as it enters the bloodstream (hence the term 'blood lactate'). These hydrogen ions are picked up by the bicarbonate ion, which exists in the blood, and then expelled from the body. The remaining compound is lactate.

Onset of blood lactate accumulation (OBLA)

Q1 At what value does OBLA occur (in mmol/litre of blood)?

Q2 What effect does the accumulation of lactic acid have on the pH of the muscle and blood?

Q3 OBLA can be described as the percentage of VO_2max used before the onset of fatigue. True or false?

Q4 For approximately how long can exercise be sustained beyond OBLA?

ANSWERS

the point at which lactate begins to
accumulate in the blood

A1 OBLA occurs at 4 mmol/litre of blood

A2 It causes the pH to decrease — a value closer to 1 means a
substance is more acidic

A3 True

A4 1 minute, since the dramatic increase in lactic acid causes acute
muscle fatigue

***examiner's* note** OBLA is sometimes referred to as the lactate or anaerobic
threshold. In trained performers, OBLA will occur at a higher percentage of
their aerobic capacity (VO$_2$max) because they can tolerate higher levels of
lactic acid and have an increased rate of lactic acid removal, meaning that it
accumulates more slowly.

Aerobic system

Q1 How much ATP can be resynthesised by means of the aerobic energy system during exercise?

Q2 Name the specialised structures within which the aerobic process takes place.

Q3 Precisely where in the mitochondria do (a) the Krebs cycle and (b) the electron transport system occur?

Q4 Complete the equation:
$$C_6H_{12}O_6 + 6O_2 \rightarrow \text{energy (ATP)} + \text{............} + \text{............}$$

ANSWERS ▶▶

A1 36 molecules (34 via the electron transport system and 2 via the Krebs cycle). An additional 2 molecules are produced during glycolysis

A2 Mitochondria

A3 (a) The matrix of the mitochondria
(b) The cristae of the mitochondria

A4 $6CO_2 + 6H_2O$

***examiner's* note** Mitochondria are central to the efficiency of the aerobic system. They can be viewed as factories that produce the end product of energy using the raw materials of glycogen, fatty acids and oxygen. Like all other factories, mitochondria can benefit from 'economies of scale'. Through endurance training, the mitochondria of the athlete increase in both size and number and become much more efficient, increasing total energy output and ATP resynthesis.

(59) **ANSWERS**

Mitochondria

Q1 With which energy system do we most associate mitochondria?

Q2 The m............... is the part of the mitochondria where the Krebs cycle takes place.

Q3 Mitochondrial density is greatest in type 2 muscle fibres. True or false?

Q4 A period of endurance-based training can stimulate divisions within existing mitochondria and increase the total number of mitochondria within muscles. True or false?

ANSWERS

the 'powerhouses' of cells, which play a central role in ATP production under aerobic conditions

A1 Aerobic system

A2 Matrix

A3 False. It is greatest in slow-twitch fibres (type 1)

A4 True. Some studies have shown mitochondrial density to increase by 100% and each mitochondrion to increase in size by up to 40%

***examiner's* note** The highest concentration of mitochondria can be found in cardiac tissue. Consequently, cardiac muscle has a very high capacity for aerobic respiration and can extract up to 80% of oxygen from the blood when at rest. (Remember that resting skeletal muscle extracts as little as 25% oxygen from the blood.)

Metabolic enzymes

Q1 Which enzyme is used in the release of energy from ATP?

Q2 Name the chief enzyme used in the release of energy from fatty acids.

Q3 Which enzyme catalyses the formation of lactate from pyruvate?

Q4 GP (glycogen phosphorylase) is an enzyme used in the release of energy from glycogen, but what exactly does it do?

ANSWERS

specialised proteins used in the production of energy

A1 ATPase

A2 Lipase

A3 Lactate dehydrogenase

A4 GP catalyses the production of glucose from glycogen

examiner's **note** Enzymes can speed up chemical reactions significantly, but only function within a narrow temperature and pH range, outside of which they can lose their structure and become denatured. The production of lactic acid when exercising can therefore denature metabolic enzymes, limiting any further production of energy.

Energy continuum

Q1 At what point during exercise does the ATP/PC–lactic acid threshold occur?

Q2 Which energy system is used predominantly during a gymnastic routine?

Q3 We tend to use the aerobic energy system as the intensity of exercise increases. True or false?

Q4 With which system is steady-state exercise most associated?

ANSWERS

the relative proportions of each energy system used during a particular activity

A1 Between 8 and 10 seconds

A2 Lactic acid system

A3 False. The higher the intensity, the more we rely upon anaerobic means of energy production (i.e. the ATP/PC and lactic acid systems)

A4 Aerobic system

***examiner's* note** When designing a training regime, a coach must first determine the relative proportions of each energy system in operation during the activity. For example, during a 400m run these are: 15% ATP/PC, 65% lactic acid, 20% aerobic. Only then can he/she plan appropriate schedules that stress the relevant energy systems and will hopefully lead to physiological adaptations that improve performance.

Fatigue

Q1 Which of the following does not contribute to muscle fatigue: hydrogen ion accumulation; decreased availability of calcium; glycogen depletion; fat metabolism?

Q2 With reference to muscle fatigue, what does DOMS stand for?

Q3 Type 2b muscle fibres are more easily exhausted than type 2a. True or false?

Q4 With reference to marathon running, explain what is meant by 'hitting the wall'.

ANSWERS

feelings of muscular tiredness that can lead to decrements in muscular performance

A1 Fat metabolism

A2 Delayed onset of muscle soreness

A3 True. These are pure fast-twitch fibres (FTG); type 2a fibres pick up some characteristics of slow-twitch fibres and thus can delay fatigue

A4 Feelings linked with muscle glycogen depletion, often in endurance events. Fatty acids can only be used in conjunction with glycogen; once glycogen is completely depleted, the body tries to metabolise fat as its only fuel source, which is difficult, and this can cause problems with muscle contraction

examiner's **note** Appropriate hydration is vital in the avoidance of fatigue. Dehydration by as little as 2% of body weight can have a detrimental effect upon performance and a 5% loss can cause performance to drop by up to 40%.

Recovery I

Q1 What does OBLA stand for?

Q2 Some athletes drink a solution of bicarbonate of soda prior to exercise in order to speed up the recovery process. How is this commonly referred to?

Q3 What terms are the two stages of recovery known by?

Q4 The o............ d............ is the amount of extra oxygen that would have been required to complete the exercise if all the energy could have been supplied aerobically.

ANSWERS

the return of the body to its pre-exercise state, or the period of adaptation between training sessions

A1 Onset of blood lactate accumulation

A2 Soda loading — the bicarbonate ion is said to improve the buffering capacity of the blood, removing lactic acid at a much quicker rate

A3 The fast component of EPOC, or alactacid debt; the slow component of EPOC, or lactacid debt

A4 Oxygen deficit

***examiner's* note** Traditionally, the term 'oxygen debt' has been used to explain the recovery process. However, this does not take into account the extra oxygen required during recovery to keep heart and respiratory rates elevated. Consequently, EPOC is the favoured term, and oxygen debt is just one aspect of this process.

Recovery II

Q1 Full recovery cannot be achieved until glycogen stores are completely recovered, which can take up to 48 hours. True or false?

Q2 What is the importance of the bicarbonate ion during recovery?

Q3 Which of the following is not an effect of lactic acid: inhibits glycolysis; acts on the pain receptors; promotes fat metabolism; impedes muscle contraction?

Q4 Does oxygen debt or EPOC always equal the oxygen deficit?

ANSWERS

the return of the body to its pre-exercise state, or the period of adaptation between training sessions

A1 True. For full recovery to occur, the body must be returned to its pre-exercise state

A2 It is the body's natural way of maintaining the acid–base balance — it mops up hydrogen ions released from lactic acid in the blood and therefore controls acidity

A3 Promotes fat metabolism

A4 No — often EPOC/oxygen debt is greater, since oxygen is needed for the recovery process itself, maintaining heart and respiratory rates

examiner's note Repayment of the slow component of EPOC (lactacid debt) can be accelerated by following a cool-down after exercise. A cool-down maintains metabolic activity, keeping heart and respiratory rates elevated, and therefore aids the faster removal of waste products such as lactic acid.

 **ANSWERS**

Excess post-exercise oxygen consumption (EPOC)

Q1 What is oxygen used for during the fast component of EPOC?

Q2 Which of the following activities is most likely to accrue a large, slow component of EPOC: 100 m sprint; 400 m run; 5 km jog; 1500 m swim?

Q3 How long does the fast component of EPOC normally take?

Q4 Lactic acid is removed in several ways. Name two fates of lactic acid.

ANSWERS

A1 Resynthesis of adenosine triphosphate (ATP) and phosphocreatine (PC); restoration of the oxy-myoglobin link

A2 400 m run — more lactic acid will accumulate during this activity

A3 Approximately 2–3 minutes

A4 Choose from: converted into CO_2 and H_2O (65%); converted into muscle and liver glycogen (20%); converted into protein (10%); converted into blood glucose (5%); small amounts may be sweated or urinated out of the body

***examiner's* note** Knowledge of EPOC is essential to the coach and athlete in the design of training programmes and sessions. For example, this knowledge can help in determining resting periods during interval training and in formulating effective microcycles where hard sessions, which require longer recovery, are perhaps followed by easier sessions.

Aerobic fitness

Q1 Which one of the following does not contribute to aerobic fitness: slow-twitch muscle fibres; phosphocreatine stores; mitochondrial density; myoglobin stores?

Q2 The PWC170 test is a test of aerobic capacity. True or false?

Q3 Give an accurate definition of VO_2max.

Q4 Which is more important in determining aerobic fitness: training or genetics?

ANSWERS

the ability to perform exercise over an extended period of time in the presence of oxygen

A1 Phosphocreatine stores

A2 True. It is a sub-maximal test which can predict VO_2max

A3 The maximum volume of oxygen that can be taken in, then transported to and consumed by the working muscles, per minute

A4 Genetics — some studies have shown VO_2max to be up to 93% genetically determined while training can only increase VO_2max by 10–20%

***examiner's* note** Aerobic fitness is a combination of cardiovascular endurance and muscular endurance. The term is often used interchangeably with the terms 'aerobic capacity' and 'maximal oxygen uptake'.

Maximum oxygen uptake (VO_2max)

Q1 State the units of VO_2max.

Q2 Which of the following is not a recognised test of VO_2max: PWC170 test; Wingate cycle test; multi-stage fitness test; Cooper 12-minute run test?

Q3 By approximately how much can training increase VO_2max scores?

Q4 Give two physiological reasons why VO_2max values are generally higher for males than for females from similar activity groups.

ANSWERS ▶▶

the maximum volume of oxygen that can be used by the working muscles in 1 minute

A1 ml/kg/min (for weight-bearing activities such as running) or litres/min (for non-weight-bearing activities such as swimming or cycling)

A2 Wingate cycle test — this is more a test of anaerobic capacity

A3 Training can only increase VO_2max by about 10–20%

A4 Choose from: males have higher haemoglobin levels; a larger heart; higher maximal cardiac output values; a lower percentage of body fat

***examiner's* note** The average active 18-year-old female has a VO_2max value of about 40 ml/kg/min. A similar 18-year-old male has a value of 48–50 ml/kg/min. The highest male score ever recorded is 94 ml/kg/min and the highest female score is 77 ml/kg/min. It is interesting to note that both scores were recorded by cross-country skiers.

Testing aerobic fitness

Q1 Which test is the most objective measurement of aerobic fitness?

Q2 The PWC170 test is a sub-maximal test of aerobic capacity. What do the letters PWC represent?

Q3 Give two disadvantages of using the multi-stage fitness test as a test of aerobic fitness.

Q4 What is the underlying premise of the PWC170 test?

ANSWERS))

A1 Direct gas analysis

A2 Physical work capacity

A3 Choose from: the test is only a prediction; it is a maximal test; it is more relevant to activities involving running (not swimmers, cyclists or rowers, for example)

A4 That heart rate and exercise intensity are linearly related

***examiner's* note** The units of measurement for VO_2max, the key measure of aerobic fitness, are ml/kg/min for weight-bearing activities such as running, and l/min for non- or partial weight-bearing activities such as cycling.

Strength I

Q1 The h............ d............ is one method of measuring an athlete's strength.

Q2 What does 1RM stand for?

Q3 Name three different types of strength.

Q4 What type of strength do we associate mostly with a triple jumper or sprinter?

ANSWERS

A1 Handgrip dynamometer

A2 One repetition maximum

A3 Choose from: maximum strength; elastic strength (explosive strength); strength endurance; static strength; dynamic strength

A4 Elastic strength — in sprinting, the muscles need to recoil rapidly in order to prepare for subsequent contractions

***examiner's* note** Gains in strength resulting from resistance training appear to be a result of two main factors. The first relates to neural adaptations, which enable the muscle to recruit more motor units. The second concerns muscle fibre hypertrophy (enlargement), which results from an increase in size and number of myofibrils per fibre.

Strength II

Q1 Male muscle tissue can produce more force than female muscle tissue. True or false?

Q2 Identify a test of elastic strength.

Q3 Give two neural adaptations to strength training.

Q4 What type of muscle fibre do you associate with strength endurance?

ANSWERS

the application of a force against a resistance

A1 False. There is no difference between male and female tissue. Males just tend to have more of it!

A2 Choose from: vertical jump test; 25 m hop test; Wingate cycle test

A3 Choose from: increased recruitment of fast-twitch muscle fibres; increased recruitment of motor units; improved coordination of motor unit recruitment

A4 Type 2a (FOG), type 1 (SO)

***examiner's* note** Plyometrics is an excellent method of training that can be used to develop elastic/explosive strength. Typically this involves jumping, hopping and bounding movements, which pre-load the target muscle with an eccentric muscle contraction before allowing a powerful concentric contraction to take place.

Strength (muscular) endurance

Q1 Strength endurance is partly dependent upon the body's ability to buffer lactic acid. True or false?

Q2 Which two muscle fibre types are most suited to endurance tasks?

Q3 Which of these tests does *not* assess strength endurance: Wingate cycle; abdominal conditioning; press-up; 1RM?

Q4 Starting with the greatest, place the following in the correct order of strength endurance requirement: high jumper; trampolinist performing a routine; rower; high diver.

ANSWERS

A1 True. This will help to delay the onset of fatigue

A2 Type 1 (slow-twitch); type 2a (FOG — fast oxidative glycolytic)

A3 1RM test — this is a test for maximum strength

A4 Rower; trampolinist; high jumper; high diver

examiner's **note** Explanations for the improvement in endurance capabilities of the muscles following a period of appropriate training centre on muscle fibre types. Research suggests that endurance training can result in type 2b (FTG) fibres being converted into type 2a (FOG). These type 2a fibres take on some characteristics of slow-twitch fibres and therefore enhance endurance capacity. This goes some way to explaining the phrase 'endurance kills speed'.

Testing strength

Q1 Give two tests of maximal strength.

Q2 For testing which of the dimensions of strength might you use the 25 m hop test?

Q3 What are the advantages of using the Wingate cycle test as a test of strength?

Q4 The abdominal conditioning test is used to assess which aspect of strength?

ANSWERS))

the assessment of strength

A1 1RM test; handgrip dynamometer

A2 Elastic strength

A3 Choose from: it provides objective data; many different aspects of strength can be assessed (e.g. peak power, time to peak power, overall power and fatigue index); high validity and reliability

A4 Strength endurance

***examiner's* note** Power is a key element in many sporting activities. Power is the rate at which strength is applied and can be thought of as explosive strength. Power can be assessed using the Wingate cycle test, sergeant jump or standing broad jump.

Strength training

Q1 Plyometrics is likely to improve which aspect of strength?

Q2 Give two types of training that you could use to improve strength endurance.

Q3 At what percentage of your 1RM would you advise training for maximum strength?

Q4 With reference to weight training, what is meant by the term 'super-setting'?

ANSWERS

A1 Elastic or explosive strength

A2 Weight training; circuit training

A3 85–100%

A4 Super-setting is a method in which you do two exercises, one after the other, with no rest in between. It can be for the same muscle group, different muscles or for opposing muscle groups

examiner's **note** In your exam, consider the link between the different dimensions of strength and the energy systems. Maximum strength, for example, uses just the breakdown of ATP to supply the necessary energy; elastic strength will primarily use the ATP-PC system; strength endurance will engage the lactic acid and aerobic systems to provide the required energy.

Plyometrics

Q1 For plyometrics to be effective, the active muscle must first have gone through an isometric contraction. True or false?

Q2 Give an example of a plyometrics exercise for the upper body.

Q3 The s............ r............ partly explains how plyometrics works and is initiated in order to prevent muscle damage.

Q4 Plyometrics training cannot be used to develop which of the following: power; speed; strength; flexibility?

ANSWERS

A1 False. The muscle must first have gone through an eccentric contraction

A2 Choose from: press-ups with claps; chest-passing a medicine ball

A3 Stretch reflex

A4 Flexibility

examiner's **note** Where possible, plyometrics training should be undertaken on a 'forgiving' surface: a sprung floor, grass or even mats. Adolescents should avoid plyometrics because the excessive loading can damage the growth plates deep inside long bones.

Power

Q1 Power is simply a combination of strength and speed. True or false?

Q2 Which of the following is not a recognised test to measure power: Wingate cycle test; abdominal conditioning test; Margaria stair climb test; vertical jump test?

Q3 Which energy system is most likely to be used by a power athlete?

Q4 P............... is one method of training used to develop power.

ANSWERS

A1 True. It is the rate at which we apply strength

A2 Abdominal conditioning test — this is a test of strength endurance

A3 ATP/PC system

A4 Plyometrics

***examiner's* note** There are some key points to remember when training using weights for optimal power development. First, the movement and contraction phase must be explosive in order to ensure that the muscle works rapidly. Second, the use of a high load is required, which will encourage the muscle to recruit more motor units. Finally, it is essential that the muscle recovers fully between sets, so that the ATP/PC system can work at maximal levels.

Flexibility

Q1 Which of the following does not affect an athlete's flexibility: elasticity of ligaments and tendons; shape of the articulating bones; type of muscle fibre surrounding the joint; type of joint?

Q2 Name a fitness test commonly used to measure flexibility.

Q3 P............. n............. f............. is one method used to develop flexibility.

Q4 Flexibility training is best performed at the beginning of a training session. True or false?

ANSWERS

the range of movement possible at a joint

A1 Type of muscle fibre surrounding the joint

A2 Choose from: sit-and-reach test; measurement of joint angles with the use of a goniometer

A3 Proprioceptive neuromuscular facilitation (PNF)

A4 False. It is best to complete any form of flexibility training at the *end* of a session, when the muscles are fully warm

***examiner's* note** During a warm-up, it is essential that the performer undertakes both static and dynamic stretching activities. Static stretching is mainly concerned with lengthening the muscle, while dynamic stretching takes the muscle through its greatest range of movement as required by the game or activity.

Proprioceptive neuromuscular facilitation (PNF)

Q1 PNF is a form of passive stretching. True or false?

Q2 Name the two types of proprioceptor involved in PNF.

Q3 One method of PNF is commonly known as the CRAC method. What does CRAC stand for?

Q4 For best results, PNF should be done without a warm-up, when the muscle is at its normal resting length. True or false?

ANSWERS

a stretching technique used to develop flexibility and mobility

A1 True. PNF requires the assistance of a partner

A2 Muscle spindle apparatus; Golgi tendon organs

A3 Contract (hold), relax, agonist contract

A4 False. All forms of mobility training are best completed at the end of a training session, when the muscle is fully warm

***examiner's* note** PNF seeks to override the stretch reflex that occurs when a muscle is stretched to its limit, so that a greater stretch can occur. The voluntary contraction of the muscle by the performer mimics the action of the stretch reflex and fools the brain into thinking that the stretch reflex has actually occurred.

Body composition

Q1 The average percentage of body fat of an 18-year-old female is between 14% and 17%. True or false?

Q2 E_____ refers to the relative pear-shapedness of the body.

Q3 Which of the following are recognised measures of body composition: body mass index; hydrostatic weighing; skin fold measure; bioelectric impedance?

Q4 The layer of subcutaneous fat is better known as a_____ t_____.

ANSWERS

A1 False. This is the range for an 18-year-old *male*; the average for an 18-year-old female is between 24% and 29%

A2 Endomorphy

A3 All of them!

A4 Adipose tissue

***examiner's* note** Each sport has an ideal body composition, but it is generally thought that high body fat hinders performance. In the control of body weight, it is therefore worth remembering the energy equation. Quite simply, if we are seeking to lose weight, then energy input (calories taken in from food) should be less than energy output (calories expended through exercise).

Testing body composition

Q1 Name two tests of body composition.

Q2 How would you calculate your body mass index?

Q3 Briefly outline bioelectric impedance as a test of body composition.

Q4 Hydrostatic weighing is recognised as the most accurate measure of body composition, but why is it not used more widely?

ANSWERS

the assessment of body fat relative to lean body mass

A1 Hydrostatic weighing, bioelectric impedance, body mass index, skinfold measurement

A2 $\text{BMI} = \dfrac{\text{weight in kilograms}}{(\text{height in metres})^2}$

A3 A small electrical current is passed through the body. Fat offers more resistance to the current than muscle tissue. When the figure derived from this is set against the height and weight of the subject, the percentage of body fat can be calculated

A4 It requires a large water tank to submerge the subject, and some subjects may suffer anxiety from immersion in water

***examiner's* note** Do not confuse scores of body fat percentage and body mass index — the units of measurement are different. A healthy percentage of body fat for an average male ranges between 14 and 17%, while for females it is between 24 and 29%. A BMI of 29, however, would class an individual as severely overweight. The BMI unit is kg/m², while body fat percentage is obviously measured as a percentage.

Obesity

Q1 One way of assessing obesity is using the body mass index. What is the critical value that defines obesity?

Q2 State three health consequences of obesity.

Q3 What type of energy balance is required to treat or combat obesity?

Q4 At what intensity of exercise is the fat-burning zone at its optimal level?

ANSWERS ▶▶

an excessive accumulation of body fat

A1 $30 \, kg/m^2$

A2 Choose from: atherosclerosis; arteriosclerosis; coronary heart disease; stroke; diabetes; gall bladder disease; bowel cancer

A3 A negative energy balance, where energy expenditure exceeds energy input

A4 Between 55 and 75%VO_2max, or 65–85%HRmax

***examiner's* note** Although widely used, the body mass index may not be the best assessment of body composition and obesity as it fails to differentiate between fat mass and muscle mass. Consequently, lean muscular athletes may well be classed as overweight or even obese!

Principles of training I

Q1 The principle of training that can be summarised as 'use it or lose it' is used to counteract r................

Q2 Which principle of training suggests that the training must stress the relevant energy system?

Q3 What does FITT stand for?

Q4 The K................ p................ uses heart rate to gauge the correct intensity of training.

ANSWERS ▶▶

rules or laws that underpin the effectiveness of a training regime

A1 Reversibility or regression

A2 Specificity

A3 Frequency, intensity, time, type

A4 Karvonen principle

***examiner's* note** Perhaps the most important principle of all is that of specificity. The specificity of training relates not only to the type of training used but also, for example, to the type of energy system in operation, the muscle fibre type used and the replication of joint actions.

Principles of training II

Q1 This principle might help in the prevention of overtraining.

Q2 This principle is followed when we gradually increase the intensity of training.

Q3 State how an athlete's maximal heart rate can be calculated.

Q4 The r............ e............ r............ is one method of determining the intensity of training, by examining which energy-providing nutrient is being predominantly used during training.

ANSWERS

A1 Moderation

A2 Progression

A3 Maximal heart rate = 220 – age

A4 Respiratory exchange ratio

examiner's **note** The respiratory exchange ratio (respiratory quotient) is calculated by dividing the volume of carbon dioxide expired per minute by the volume of oxygen consumed per minute. The closer the result is to 1.0, the more we are relying on glycogen as our predominant food fuel, which signifies a higher workload. A value of, say, 0.7 suggests that the predominant fuel is fatty acids and that the exercise is of lower intensity.

Warm-up

Q1 State two effects of adrenaline on the cardiovascular system.

Q2 A warm-up can be classed as a principle of training. True or false?

Q3 Which of the following is the correct order in which a warm-up should be performed: (a) pulse raiser, stretching, skills; (b) stretching, skills, pulse raiser; (c) stretching, pulse raiser, skills

Q4 The relative resistance to blood flow is known as b............... v...............

ANSWERS

A1 Choose from: increases the heart rate; dilates capillaries; decreases the viscosity of the blood

A2 True. A warm-up (and cool-down) should be completed prior to (and after) every training session

A3 (a) Pulse raiser, stretching, skills

A4 Blood viscosity

***examiner's* note** A skills-based section of a warm-up for a volleyball player may include the following: throwing and catching the ball with a partner to warm up the shoulders; digging and volleying the ball with a partner; feed, dig, set and spike in a group of four; serving practice.

Types of training I

Q1 What does SAQ stand for in relation to methods of training?

Q2 Fartlek is a type of continuous training. True or false?

Q3 When developing maximum strength, what should the intensity of the training load be (approximately)?

Q4 Which of the following training methods would not benefit a 100 m sprinter: altitude training; interval training; resistance training; mobility training?

ANSWERS ▶▶

A1 Speed, agility and quickness

A2 True

A3 85–100% of 1RM

A4 Altitude training — this is of more benefit to the endurance athlete

***examiner's* note** SAQ (speed, agility and quickness) is a relatively new method of training that seeks to develop multi-directional strength and power, efficiency of neuromuscular coordination and reaction time. It is commonly used in invasion games, owing to the need to change direction quickly in these activities. Plyometrics, slalom runs and ladder drills are all examples of SAQ exercises.

Types of training II

Q1 With what type of training would you associate the term 'depth jumping'?

Q2 Within what range should the heart rate of an elite endurance athlete be when in the training zone? (Hint: your answer should refer to a percentage of maximal heart rate.)

Q3 Repetitions, sets and recovery periods are characteristic of what type of training?

Q4 A Swiss ball is predominantly used to develop c.............. s...............

ANSWERS

methods that stress and aim to improve each component of fitness

A1 Plyometrics

A2 70–85% of maximal heart rate

A3 Interval training

A4 Core stability

***examiner's* note** Circuit training is particularly good for general body conditioning. However, it is necessary for the circuit to be designed to meet the specific fitness requirements of the sport in question. A squash player should therefore expect plenty of agility and lunging exercises, while a rugby player can expect some exercises that involve contact with tackle bags and shields, since these actions replicate movements from the respective sports.

Interval training

Q1 Interval training can be used to improve both aerobic and anaerobic fitness. True or false?

Q2 The recovery period of interval training, expressed as a percentage of the work period, is the w............:r............ r............

Q3 Typically, does the number of repetitions increase or decrease when the aerobic system is stressed?

Q4 When stressing the ATP/PC (alactic) system, which type of recovery is suggested: work relief or rest relief?

ANSWERS

A1 True

A2 Work:relief ratio

A3 Decrease

A4 Rest relief — this ensures full recovery, which is desirable when stressing the ATP/PC system

***examiner's* note** Interval training is a versatile type of training and variables can be manipulated in order to stress aerobic or anaerobic energy systems. The main variables that can be changed are: the distance/duration of the work interval; the intensity of the work interval; the number of repetitions; the number of sets; the duration of the rest interval.

Health-related fitness programme

Q1 What does PAR-Q stand for? Why is it important?

Q2 How is the body mass index calculated?

Q3 Regular exercise can reduce the effects of adult-onset diabetes. True or false?

Q4 The rate at which the body uses energy is known as the m............... r...............

ANSWERS

an exercise programme designed specifically to improve health and rehabilitate individuals

A1 Physical activity readiness questionnaire; it should be used to screen individuals before prescribing an exercise programme

A2 BMI $= \dfrac{\text{weight in kilograms}}{(\text{height in metres})^2}$

A3 True. Exercise increases the breakdown of blood glucose

A4 Metabolic rate

***examiner's* note** Exercise can reduce the overall risk of developing cardiovascular disease by about 30%, not only as a result of cardiovascular adaptation but also by inducing the 'feel-good factor' and reducing stress.

Periodisation I

Q1 Name the three phases of a periodised year.

Q2 A macrocycle is usually 1 year in length. True or false?

Q3 In order to prevent overtraining, athletes should follow the principle of hard:easy. At what ratio?

Q4 During the initial phase of pre-season training for a games player, which of the following is the most important component of fitness to stress: aerobic endurance; strength; speed; power?

ANSWERS

the organisation of the training year into phases, in order to peak for competition

A1 Preparation; competition; transition

A2 True — but can be more, even as much as 4 years

A3 3:1, i.e. three hard weeks followed by one easy week, or three hard sessions followed by one easy session

A4 Aerobic endurance — this is the foundation on which to build all other aspects of fitness

***examiner's* note** Before planning your periodised year, you must first decide when the competitive season begins or when the competition for which you are training takes place. The periodised year for a netball player might look something like this:

JUL AUG SEP	OCT NOV DEC JAN FEB MAR APR	MAY JUN
Preparation	Competition	Transition

Periodisation II

Q1 How long does a microcycle typically last?

Q2 When might athletes follow a double-periodised year? Give an example.

Q3 The process of decreasing the volume yet maintaining the intensity of training as competition approaches is known as t...............

Q4 A megacycle is sometimes used to describe a training cycle of 4 years, e.g. when athletes are preparing for an Olympic Games. True or false?

ANSWERS

A1 1 week — but it can be slightly shorter or longer, depending upon the activity

A2 When they need to peak twice in a season, e.g. indoor and outdoor season in athletics

A3 Tapering

A4 True

***examiner's* note** A double-periodised year might be necessary when a performer is required to peak twice in a year. An obvious example is that of a track-and-field athlete needing to peak for an indoor and an outdoor event. In this instance, the periodised year might look something like this:

OCT NOV DEC	JAN	FEB	MAR APR MAY	JUN JUL AUG	SEP
Preparation	Comp	Trans	Preparation	Competition	Trans

Adaptive response I

Q1 C............ h............ is the term used to describe the increased size of the heart following a period of training.

Q2 The resting value of cardiac output of an athlete is greater than that of a non-athlete. True or false?

Q3 Which of the following types of training is most likely to increase myoglobin content: weight training; sprint interval training; continuous training; plyometrics?

Q4 Endurance training can increase VO_2max by 50%. True or false?

ANSWERS

long-term physiological change that occurs in the body as a result of training

A1 Cardiac hypertrophy

A2 False. Cardiac output is the same at rest

A3 Continuous training

A4 False. Studies show that VO_2max can only be increased by 10–20% as a result of training

***examiner's* note** Adaptation depends on the type of prior training. Anaerobic adaptation usually occurs as a result of sprint interval training, high-intensity resistance training and plyometrics. Aerobic adaptation results from continuous training and endurance-based interval training.

Adaptive response II

Q1 What is bradycardia?

Q2 Anaerobic training can improve the b............... capacity of the muscle and blood, enabling them to deal effectively with lactic acid.

Q3 An increase in which of these would be most likely following a period of plyometrics training: PC stores; mitochondrial density; capillarisation; size of type 1 muscle fibres?

Q4 Endurance training can significantly increase lung volume. True or false?

ANSWERS ▶▶

A1 Literally meaning 'slow heart', it is used to denote a resting heart rate of below 60 bpm, which accompanies endurance training

A2 Buffering

A3 PC stores

A4 False. Lung volumes are only slightly increased as a result of endurance training

***examiner's* note** Miguel Indurain, one of the world's best Tour de France cyclists, is reported to have had a resting heart rate of 28 bpm. This incredibly low figure would have allowed Indurain's heart rate to increase substantially during exercise. Having such a large heart rate range enables cardiac output to increase to up to 50 litres/minute.

Ergogenic aid I

Q1 All ergogenic aids are illegal. True or false?

Q2 Give one possible risk of blood doping.

Q3 Which two of the following performers are most likely to use diuretics: judo player; marathon runner; cyclist; jockey?

Q4 Name the designer drug that has recently blighted athletics, first appearing in the world championships of 2003 and resulting in a ban being imposed on Dwain Chambers?

ANSWERS

a substance, object or training method used to enhance athletic performance

A1 False — some are perfectly legal, e.g. nasal strips, altitude training

A2 Choose from: increased blood viscosity; increased risk of blood clots; increased risk of heart failure; blood contamination

A3 Judo player and jockey — diuretics are commonly used in weight control when performers must not exceed a certain weight

A4 Tetrahydrogestrinone (THG)

***examiner's* note** The risks involved in using anabolic steroids are considerable. Liver damage and cardiovascular disease are common, as is 'roid rage' — a personality disorder. In men, testicular atrophy (reduced testicle size), a reduced sperm count and development of breasts have all been noted; women tend to develop more masculine features and may experience disruption of their menstrual cycle.

 ANSWERS

Ergogenic aid II

Q1 What term is used to describe the synthetic form of erythropoietin (EPO)?

Q2 H.......... g.......... h.......... is a type of ergogenic aid that stimulates protein and nucleic acid synthesis in muscle.

Q3 Name the five categories of ergogenic aid that have been identified.

Q4 M.......... a.......... hide banned substances that otherwise may show up in urine samples.

ANSWERS

a substance, object or training method used
to enhance athletic performance

A1 Recombinant erythropoietin (rhEPO)

A2 Human growth hormone

A3 Pharmacological; mechanical; physiological; nutritional;
psychological

A4 Masking agents

***examiner's* note** Colostrum is fast becoming a favoured nutritional
supplement for athletes. It is derived from the pre-milk fluid produced by
pregnant cows. Research conducted into colostrum has shown benefits to
growth and development of muscle, skeletal and nerve tissue, and immune
benefits, which help the body fight off harmful invaders such as viruses and
bacteria.

Altitude training

Q1 The percentage of oxygen in the air at high altitude is the same as at sea level. True or false?

Q2 Which of the following is most likely to benefit from altitude training: strength athlete; power athlete; endurance athlete?

Q3 It is possible to create a hypobaric (low-pressure) environment at sea level. True or false?

Q4 Exercise physiologists believe that the best way to maximise the effects of altitude is to live and train at altitude. True or false?

ANSWERS

training in hypobaric environments, causing the body to adapt by increasing red blood cell mass

A1 True. The percentage of oxygen remains the same (20.93%); it is the partial pressure of oxygen that decreases with altitude

A2 Endurance athlete

A3 True. Hypobaric chambers recreate the low-pressure conditions found at altitude

A4 False. They suggest living at altitude but training at sea level

examiner's note The debate is continuing on the effectiveness of altitude training, since the proposed benefits come at a cost, both financial and physiological. Altitude sickness may be a problem and performers are often too tired to train and physically cannot exercise very hard when they do. This is in addition to the associated travelling and living expenses.

Glycogen loading

Q1 Which of the following athletes is least likely to benefit from glycogen loading: triathlete; rower; marathon runner; touring cyclist?

Q2 A glycogen-loading regime can cause muscle stiffness, fatigue and tiredness. True or false?

Q3 The use of glycogen loading or dietary manipulation to help improve performance is known as n_____ e_____ a_____.

Q4 Give a brief outline of a glycogen-loading regime.

ANSWERS

the manipulation of carbohydrate intake and exercise in order to maximise glycogen stores

A1 Rower — rowing events last around 5 minutes, so the body should have sufficient glycogen stores without the need for carbo-loading

A2 True

A3 Nutritional ergogenic aid

A4 Day 1, exhaustive exercise; days 2, 3, 4, limited carbohydrate intake; days 5, 6, 7, carbohydrate-rich diet and reduced training intensity; day 8, competition

***examiner's* note** Recent research suggests that the initial depletion phase of glycogen loading may not be necessary. Instead, athletes should reduce the intensity of training 7 days before the competition while maintaining a mixed diet containing 55–60% carbohydrates. Three days prior to the competition, training is more or less stopped and a carbohydrate-rich diet consumed.

Healthy, balanced lifestyle — injury

Q1 What is a hyperbaric chamber?

Q2 In terms of injury management, what does the acronym PRICE mean?

Q3 What types of muscle contraction are primarily associated with DOMS?

Q4 Briefly explain how ice baths work.

ANSWERS ▶▶

the prevention and management of injury to promote healthy, balanced lifestyles

A1 A chamber that delivers 100% pure oxygen at very high pressure, which promotes recovery of injured performers

A2 P = Protect; R = Rest; I = Ice; C = Compress; E = Elevate

A3 Eccentric muscle contractions

A4 Immersion in cold water causes blood vessels to constrict, draining away any waste products. Exiting the ice bath invokes a blood rush which flushes the muscle with fresh, nutrient-rich oxygenated blood

***examiner's* note** Some injured performers may use hypoxic (low-oxygen) tents when rehabilitating from an injury. This provides similar benefits to altitude training, so even if the performer is unable to train, his or her body can adapt to the low-oxygen conditions by increasing the volume of red blood cells, thereby minimising any losses in aerobic fitness.

Delayed onset of muscle soreness (DOMS)

Q1 DOMS occurs late in the exercise session. True or false?

Q2 Which form of running is most likely to cause DOMS: running downhill; running on a level surface; running uphill?

Q3 DOMS is more acute when the prior exercise has involved eccentric muscle contractions. True or false?

Q4 The amount of lactic acid accumulated during the exercise session will have an effect on DOMS. True or false?

ANSWERS

A1 False. It develops a day or two after the exercise session

A2 Running downhill

A3 True

A4 False. Lactic acid will have been removed within an hour or so of training. DOMS largely results from micro-tears in the connective tissue surrounding the muscle

***examiner's* note** Muscular pain felt during and immediately following exercise is known as 'acute muscle soreness'. It results largely from the accumulation of lactic acid and generally disappears within an hour or two of the exercise.

Motor control

Q1 Nerve cells that stimulate skeletal muscle are called m........ n..........

Q2 What is the all or none law?

Q3 What is a motor unit?

Q4 An increase in responsiveness of a nerve resulting from the additive effect of several stimuli is known as s.......... s............

ANSWERS

A1 Motor neurones

A2 The all or none law states that 'when a motor unit receives a stimulus of sufficient intensity, every muscle fibre within it will contract to its maximum possible extent'

A3 The motor nerve, together with the muscle fibres that it controls

A4 Spatial summation

examiner's note The degree to which a muscle contracts can be increased by stimulating more motor units and by increasing the rate at which impulses arrive at the motor units.